●━CONTINUOUS IMPROVEMENT TOOLS

VOLUME 1

A Practical Guide To Achieve Quality Results

Richard Y. Chang

Matthew E. Niedzwiecki

Jossey-Bass
Pfeiffer
San Francisco

RICHARD
CHANG
ASSOCIATES

Published by

Jossey-Bass
Pfeiffer

350 Sansome Street, 5th Floor
San Francisco, California 94104-1342
(415) 433-1740; Fax (415) 433-0499
(800) 274-4434; Fax (800) 569-0443

Visit our website at: www.pfeiffer.com

Printing   10   9   8   7   6   5   4   3   2   1

ACKNOWLEDGMENTS

About The Authors

Richard Y. Chang is President and CEO of Richard Chang Associates, Inc., a diversified organizational improvement consulting firm based in Irvine, California. He is internationally recognized for his management strategy, quality improvement, organization development, customer satisfaction, and human resource development expertise.

Matthew E. Niedzwiecki, Manager of Quality Management at Children's Hospital Los Angeles, is an experienced training and organization development practitioner. His extensive background and areas of expertise include total quality management, training design, process analysis, and data interpretation.

The authors would like to acknowledge the support of the entire team of professionals at Richard Chang Associates, Inc. for their contribution to the guidebook development process. In addition, special thanks are extended to the many client organizations who have helped us shape the practical ideas and proven methods shared in this guidebook.

Additional Credits

Editor:	Sarah Ortlieb Fraser
Reviewers:	Kevin Kehoe, P. Keith Kelly, Christina Slater, and Ruth Stingley
Graphic Layout:	Christina Slater
Cover Design:	John Odam Design Associates

PREFACE

The 1990's have already presented individuals and organizations with some very difficult challenges to face and overcome. So who will have the advantage as we move toward the year 2000 and beyond?

The advantage will belong to those with a commitment to continuous learning. Whether on an individual basis or as an entire organization, one key ingredient to building a continuous learning environment is *The Practical Guidebook Collection* brought to you by the Publications Division of Richard Chang Associates, Inc.

After understanding the future *"learning needs"* expressed by our clients and other potential customers, we are pleased to publish *The Practical Guidebook Collection*. These guidebooks are designed to provide you with proven, *"real-world"* tips, tools, and techniques—on a wide range of subjects—that you can apply in the workplace and/or on a personal level immediately.

Once you've had a chance to benefit from *The Practical Guidebook Collection*, please share your feedback with us. We've included a brief *Evaluation and Feedback Form* at the end of the guidebook that you can fax to us at (949) 727-7007.

With your feedback, we can continuously improve the resources we are providing through the Publications Division of Richard Chang Associates, Inc.

Wishing you successful reading,

Richard Y. Chang
President and CEO
Richard Chang Associates, Inc.

TABLE OF CONTENTS

"The single most destructive force in the move to improving the quality of American organizations today is the lack of commitment and understanding of how to make quality happen on the job."

Anonymous

CHAPTER ONE

INTRODUCTION

Total quality management. You've heard about it. You've seen much written about it. You may even be applying the concepts *(successfully or not so successfully)* right now on the job. The quality revolution is upon us, and unlike some of the other corporate revolutions you may have been through…this one's here to stay!

Why Read This Guidebook?

In today's business environment, things seem to change daily *(or hourly, in some cases)*! How do you keep up? The answer: Everyone in your organization, from the president to the hourly employee, must be committed to continuously improving all that he or she does to achieve quality on the job.

The question that has haunted organizations and individuals attempting to implement quality-improvement plans over the years still rings loud and clear: *"What can we do at work to make quality happen?"* Often, responsibility for quality gets pushed up, down, and sideways in organizations. From the boardroom to the shop floor, you can hear these echoing words: *"I can't do anything about that!"*

Who Should Read This Guidebook?

You can do something to make quality happen! The tools and techniques presented in this guidebook offer a commonsense approach that will help you *(as a front-line employee, supervisor, trainer, or executive)* not only begin, but also sustain any quality-improvement efforts *(e.g., process improvement, problem-solving teams, self-managed work teams, quality circles, etc.)* already in place in your organization.

When And How To Use It

You may use and reference this guidebook during meetings, while working on teams, or in your own work area, and anytime you have a question about which *"quality tool"* to use and/or how to use it.

This volume of *Continuous Improvement Tools* contains step-by-step instructions along with real-life examples. Included are these seven basic, yet popular and effective, planning, analysis, and interpretation tools: Brainstorming, Affinity Diagram, Matrix Diagram, Criteria Rating Form, Check Sheet, Force Field Diagram, and the Cause and Effect Diagram.

When deciding which tool to use for your situation, take a moment to look at the Selection Matrix on the next page. Whether you need a tool for planning, analysis or interpretation, you'll find these tools useful, practical, and easy to adapt for your own purposes. At the end of each chapter you'll find a worksheet to jot down ideas for using the specific tool in your organization. In addition, there are worksheets and blank reproducible forms in the Appendix for you to use on the job. Write in this guidebook, fold the pages, get it dirty, but don't let it sit on your shelf!

Continuous Improvement Tools Selection Matrix

	TOOL \ USE	Planning	Analysis	Interpretation	Team	Individual
VOLUME 1	Brainstorming	✗	✗		✗	
	Affinity Diagram	✗	✗		✗	
	Matrix Diagram	✗			✗	✗
	Force Field Diagram		✗		✗	
	Cause and Effect		✗		✗	
	Criteria Rating	✗		✗	✗	
	Check Sheet		✗	✗		✗
VOLUME 2	Tree Diagram	✗			✗	
	Pareto Chart			✗		✗
	Sequence Flow Chart	✗	✗		✗	✗
	Process Flow Chart	✗	✗		✗	✗
	Scatter Diagram			✗		✗
	Run Chart		✗	✗		✗
	Control Chart		✗	✗		✗
	Histogram		✗	✗	✗	✗

Note: In Volume 2, tools and techniques such as Pareto Charting, Process and Sequence Flowcharting, Scatter Diagrams, Run/Control Charts, and the Tree Diagram are discussed in detail.

BRAINSTORMING

Brainstorming is a planning tool you can use to tap the creativity of a group. Teams and departments should use Brainstorming when:

- ☞ **Determining possible causes and/or solutions to problems**

- ☞ **Planning out the steps of a project**

- ☞ **Deciding which problem** *(or improvement opportunity)* **to work on**

Teams often use Brainstorming as a consensus-building tool, and in situations where they need to generate a large number of ideas.

The two key steps to Brainstorming are:

STEP 1: Start the Brainstorming session

STEP 2: Determine the type of Brainstorming method to use

Now let's look at an example of how Brainstorming works in a problem-solving team at Victory, Inc.

Bob, the leader...

of a problem-solving team at Victory, Inc., thought he needed to jump-start the team to come up with new ideas on solving the age-old question of how top management could communicate more effectively. He started the session off by saying, *"Let's try to brainstorm some new ideas."* Ignoring the usual moans and grumbling about trying new methods, he launched into the Brainstorming session....

Step 1: Start The Brainstorming Session

⟶ Provide a time limit for the session. Generally, 30 minutes is sufficient.

⟶ Identify one or more Recorders. The Recorder's job is to write all ideas down *(where everyone can see them, such as on a flip chart or overhead transparency)* as they are voiced.

⟶ Establish the ground rules *(see Diagram # 1)*.

The group decided...

to brainstorm for 30 minutes. After a little gentle prodding from Bob, Denise decided to be the Recorder. As she stood at the flip chart, armed with three different-colored markers, and prepared to use her charting skills, Bob reminded the group not to criticize even the most outrageous ideas. He hoped they'd generate at least 30 ideas during the 30-minute session....

GROUND RULES

⇨ Don't edit what is said and remember not to criticize ideas.

⇨ Go for quantity of ideas at this point; narrow down the list later.

⇨ Encourage wild or exaggerated ideas (creativity is the key).

⇨ Build on the ideas of others (e.g., one member might say something that "sparks" another member's idea).

Diagram # 1 - Ground rules

Step 2: Determine The Type Of Brainstorming Method To Use

Choose either the **freewheeling** or **round robin** method of Brainstorming.

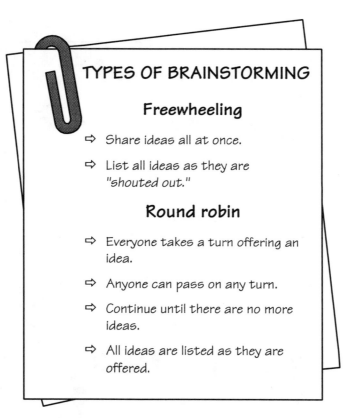

TYPES OF BRAINSTORMING

Freewheeling

⇨ Share ideas all at once.

⇨ List all ideas as they are "shouted out."

Round robin

⇨ Everyone takes a turn offering an idea.

⇨ Anyone can pass on any turn.

⇨ Continue until there are no more ideas.

⇨ All ideas are listed as they are offered.

Bob began the group's Brainstorming session by...

offering an idea that Denise promptly listed on the flip chart. After that, some more team members chimed in with ideas, and then silence fell over the group. Bob thought, *"How can we be out of ideas already?"* So, he suggested the team switch gears and use the round robin approach. He explained that each person around the table should consecutively offer an idea, or pass to the next person. This approach was more effective, and soon the members were back to *"shouting out"* ideas. Denise even had trouble keeping up, since the ideas were coming so fast. She had to ask Ted to help her record them....

Decide On Next Steps

You know it's time to end your Brainstorming session when:

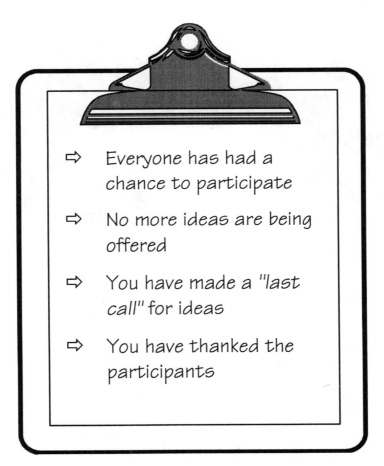

➪ Everyone has had a chance to participate

➪ No more ideas are being offered

➪ You have made a "last call" for ideas

➪ You have thanked the participants

After about half an hour...

the group ran out of ideas. Bob announced, *"last call for ideas"* Ted mischievously replied, *"Oh no, I want to go for another hour!"* Everyone laughed, and Bob knew the rag had been rung dry. He thanked all participants for their enthusiasm, and Denise and Ted for their willingness to get sore hands as recorders. The group agreed to wait until the following week to prioritize their ideas and decide on a starting point in their problem-solving process.

After you've finished Brainstorming:

➠ Prioritize your ideas to help you decide where to start.

➠ Sort large amounts of information according to common themes *(see the Affinity Diagram in the next chapter).*

➠ Remember, Brainstorming is based on people's opinions, so you may need to gather data to support or prove ideas.

In summary, use Brainstorming when:

☑ You want to determine possible causes and/or solutions to problems. *(Brainstorming helps your team generate a large quantity of ideas.)*

☑ Planning out the steps of a project. *(Although not the primary use of this tool, Brainstorming can be used to help identify the different steps in implementing a project.)*

☑ When deciding which problem *(or improvement opportunity)* to work on. *(You can use Brainstorming in any situation where many ideas need to be generated in a relatively short period of time.)*

☑ You want to include all opinions. *(Round-robin Brainstorming helps to ensure equal participation in an idea-generating session.)*

CHAPTER TWO WORKSHEET:
BRAINSTORMING—IDEAS FOR USE

1. List the specific opportunities you have in your organization to use Brainstorming.

_____

_____

_____

_____

2. Which method will work best in these situations, and why?

☐ Freewheeling. Why?

_____

_____

_____

_____

☐ Round robin. Why?

_____

_____

_____

_____

3. Which of the following ground rules should you use in the situations you listed above?

☐ No judging, evaluating or criticizing

☐ Go for quantity

☐ Be creative

☐ Build on ideas

AFFINITY DIAGRAM

You should use the Affinity Diagram as a planning tool when you want to:

- ☞ **Add structure to a large or complicated issue**

- ☞ **Break down a complicated issue into easy-to-understand categories**

- ☞ **Gain agreement on an issue or situation**

STEP 1: State the issue or problem to be worked on

STEP 2: Generate ideas for the issue in question

STEP 3: Collect the cards or sticky notes

STEP 4: Arrange the cards or sticky notes into related groups

STEP 5: Create a title or heading for each group

In the following example, a team uses the Affinity Diagram to help organize a complex issue.

Anthony is the leader of a team...

that has been asked to sit down with its organization's major customers and *"hash out"* the customers' requirements, wants, and needs. Anthony had seen the Affinity Diagram used in situations where large amounts of data needed to be organized. *"Well,"* he decided, *"this is certainly a situation where a tool like that could be helpful."*...

Step 1: State The Issue Or Problem To Be Worked On

At the start of your Affinity session:

⇒ Provide a time limit for the session. Generally, 45 to 60 minutes is sufficient.

⇒ Start with a clear, objective problem or goal statement that everyone agrees to.

Goal Statement

After the group...

(including representatives from the organization's major customers) filed in, Anthony asked all those present to introduce themselves. He announced the group's goal *(which he had written on a flip chart)*. He also said the meeting would last about an hour....

Step 2: Generate Ideas For The Issue In Question

➡ Each participant should think of ideas and write them on index cards, sticky notes, or have a Recorder write them on a flip chart.

Note: The advantage of using the flip chart is that everyone can see the ideas and build from them. See the previous chapter for Brainstorming ground rules. The disadvantage of this technique is that group members may be intimidated by this process, and not participate.

➡ The idea statements should be concisely listed in one to three words. One idea should be used per card or sticky note.

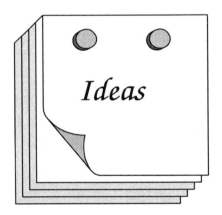
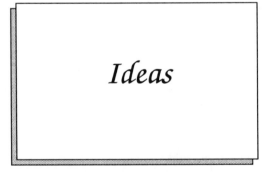

Anthony handed a stack of sticky notes...

to each participant and asked them to write their thoughts about customer requirements, wants, and needs down in short, concise statements. He reminded them to write only one idea on each sticky note. The group had some trouble getting started but after a couple of minutes, all were busily writing. Anthony gave the group 15 minutes to complete this part of the exercise....

Step 3: Collect The Cards Or Sticky Notes

➠ Collect the cards *(or sticky notes)*, mix them up and then spread them out *(or stick them)* on a flat surface.

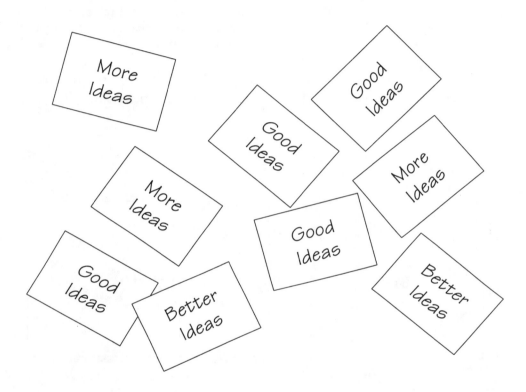

Anthony called "time,"...

and collected the ideas from the participants. He mixed them up before sticking them on the wall to ensure the ideas would remain anonymous. That way no bias would be involved—all ideas would be treated equally....

Step 4: Arrange The Cards Or Sticky Notes Into Related Groups

➠ All participants should pick out cards *(or sticky notes)* that list related ideas and set them aside. Repeat this until all of the cards *(or sticky notes)* have been placed in groupings.

Note: Don't force cards *(or sticky notes)* into groupings. There may be only one card *(or sticky note)* per grouping. In some cases you may decide not to use an idea at all *(e.g., some ideas may be duplicates)*.

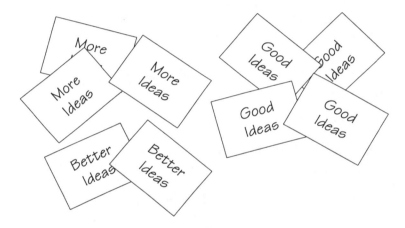

Diagram # 2 - Ideas arranged by related group

➠ This process should take about 15 minutes and works best when conversation between participants is not allowed. This encourages freethinking and discourages arguments over placement of cards *(or sticky notes)*.

After Anthony stuck all the sticky notes to the wall,...

he asked the group to arrange the ideas into related groups *(see Diagram # 2)*. Anthony asked that this be done in silence, so no one would be influenced by any other group member. As the participants began moving sticky notes around, it looked as though the ideas were being separated into four major groups....

Step 5: Create A Title Or Heading For Each Group

➠ Develop a title or heading that best describes the theme of each group of cards *(or sticky notes)*.

➠ Headings should be short *(one to three words)* and describe the main theme/focus of the group it represents.

➠ To help you see additional relationships, place groups that are similar next to each other.

➠ If groups are very similar, you can combine two or more groups to create one large group under a new title or heading.

➠ Continue this process until your team agrees on the grouping of cards.

After discussing the grouping of ideas . . .

for 15 minutes, it became obvious to the participants that four distinct categories of customer requirements had emerged. The categories were responsiveness, follow-up, service, and support. The remaining two sticky notes were grouped in a *"miscellaneous"* category *(see Diagram # 3)....*

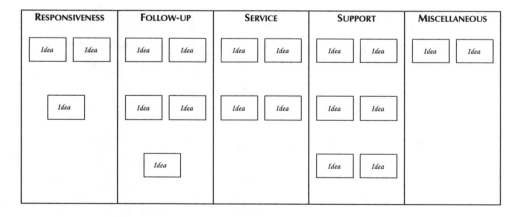

Diagram # 3 - Group the ideas and name each group

Decide On Next Steps

You know it's time to end the Affinity Diagram session when:

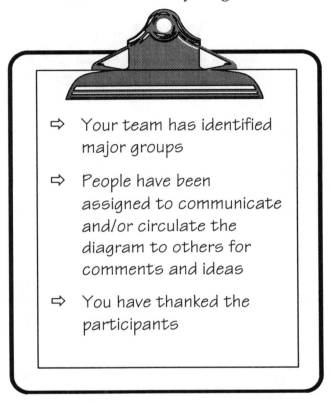

⇨ Your team has identified major groups

⇨ People have been assigned to communicate and/or circulate the diagram to others for comments and ideas

⇨ You have thanked the participants

Remember that the process of completing the Affinity Diagram is an ongoing one. It is likely that you will modify or change your diagram.

For the first time in the organization's history,...

it was clear what was important to its customers. Anthony was surprised by the number of things the customers were expecting that no one in the organization seemed to anticipate. Anthony asked Patty to circulate the final Affinity Diagram to the management team on Monday, for their feedback and input. He thanked the group for participating in the process. Lastly, he scheduled a follow-up meeting to discuss any changes to the Affinity Diagram and to identify ways to better meet the customers' requirements.

SUMMARY

In summary, use the Affinity Diagram when:

☑ You want to add structure when handling a large or complicated issue. *(The Affinity Diagram is a structured method of Brainstorming that you can use for larger, more complex activities such as developing a mission statement or a vision statement.)*

☑ You want to break down a complicated issue into easy-to-understand categories. *(An issue or problem may have several sub-issues, or may be so large that it needs to be broken down into more manageable pieces.)*

☑ You want to gain agreement on an issue or situation. *(When ideas are brainstormed individually, the Affinity Diagram is a useful tool to ensure that all team members have an equal voice).*

CHAPTER THREE WORKSHEET:
AFFINITY DIAGRAM—IDEAS FOR USE

1. List the specific opportunities you have in your organization to use the Affinity Diagram.

_____

_____

_____

_____

_____

_____

_____

2. What advantages or benefits of the Affinity Diagram would you describe to a group using it for the first time?

_____

_____

_____

_____

_____

_____

_____

MATRIX DIAGRAM

The Matrix Diagram is a planning tool that can help you to organize large groups of tasks and responsibilities.

Note: There are many types of Matrix Diagrams. We will only be looking at the L-Shaped Diagram

Use The Matrix Diagram To:

☞ **Match tasks with the individuals, departments, or functions completing them**

☞ **Show a relationship between a task and the responsible person, department, or function**

☞ **Rate the strength of that relationship**

☞ **Assign accountability and plan actions**

STEP 1: Prepare for the Matrix Diagram session

STEP 2: Agree on tasks

STEP 3: Record responsibilities

STEP 4: Rate each intersection

The example that follows illustrates a typical use of a Matrix Diagram in an administrative setting.

Christina, an Administrative Assistant,...

volunteered to lead a team responsible for updating her company's operating procedures manual. She assembled a team of five people *(who were affected by the policy)* from different departments to work on this project....

Step 1: Prepare For The Matrix Diagram Session

At the start of your Matrix Diagram session:

⇒ Create a flip chart or an overhead transparency of a Matrix Diagram *(see Diagram # 4)*.

⇒ Provide a time limit for the session. Generally, 45 to 60 minutes is sufficient.

⇒ Identify a Recorder. The job of the Recorder is to write down *(on a flip chart or overhead transparency)* tasks, responsible individuals and/or departments, and the strength of the relationship.

Christina called a meeting...

to clarify the team's mission and to decide how to tackle the project at hand. She knew that the process would be complicated, so she suggested using the Matrix Diagram. She explained that it would help them identify the tasks and responsibilities needed to complete the project. Christina drew the matrix on a flip chart and asked Paul to be the Recorder....

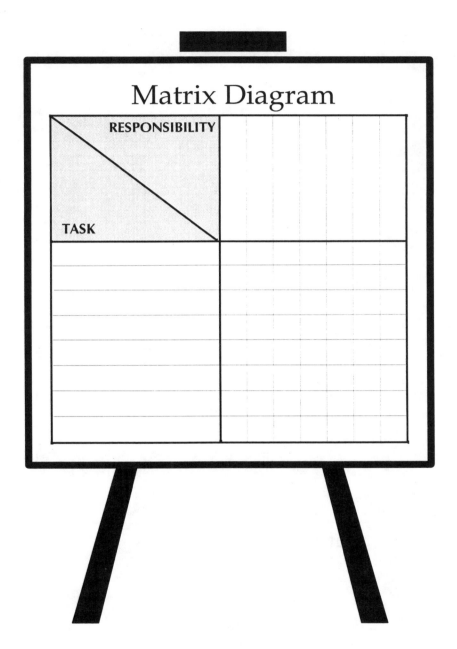

Matrix Diagram

RESPONSIBILITY

TASK

Diagram # 4 - The L-Shaped Matrix Diagram

Step 2: Agree On Tasks

➟ Write the tasks or responsibilities that your team needs to complete on the left side of the Matrix Diagram. As a group, identify the tasks that you can accomplish by Brainstorming. *(See Chapter Two for the ground rules of Brainstorming.)*

Note: The tasks and responsibilities don't have to be in sequential order.

RESPONSIBILITY / TASK							
Writing							
Proofing							
Editing							
Researching							
Binding							
Copying							
Training							
Distribution							

Diagram # 5 - Record the tasks

Christina asked the group to brainstorm a list of tasks...

they needed to complete to update the manual. The group decided on eight major tasks: writing, proofing, editing, researching, binding, copying, training, and distribution. Paul recorded all the responses on the left side of the Matrix Diagram *(see Diagram # 5)*....

Step 3: Record Responsibilities

⟶ Along the top of the Matrix Diagram, list the various individuals, departments, and/or suppliers that will complete the listed tasks or responsibilities.

After agreeing on the tasks,...

the team started to fill in the top of the Matrix Diagram with names of team members and the departments and suppliers that would be involved in the project. Each team member was listed, as was the Human Resources Department and a local printer. Once again, Paul filled out the information on the Matrix Diagram *(see Diagram # 6)*....

RESPONSIBILITY / TASK	Christina	Paul	Penny	Maria	Juan	H.R. Dept.	Printer
Writing							
Proofing							
Editing							
Researching							
Binding							
Copying							
Training							
Distribution							

Diagram # 6 - Record the responsibilities

Step 4: Rate Each Intersection

➠ For each intersection of a task and an individual, department, or supplier, assign a *"strength"* rating using the following symbols:

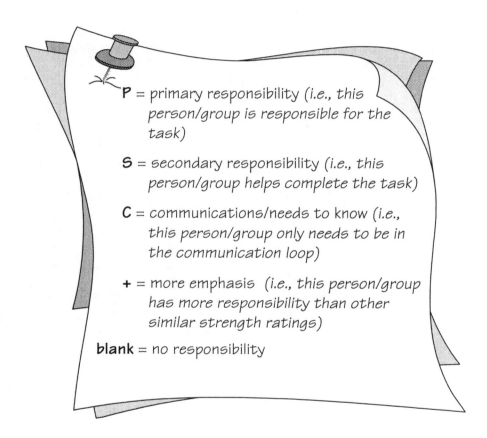

P = primary responsibility (i.e., this person/group is responsible for the task)

S = secondary responsibility (i.e., this person/group helps complete the task)

C = communications/needs to know (i.e., this person/group only needs to be in the communication loop)

+ = more emphasis (i.e., this person/group has more responsibility than other similar strength ratings)

blank = no responsibility

➠ Remember, each task must have one *(and only one)* rating of *"primary responsibility,"* since this indicates ownership of the task. The *"more emphasis"* rating is used to indicate a difference between two similar *"strength"* ratings (i.e., *if more than one person has two secondary responsibilities for a task, one might be labeled with a "+" for more emphasis*).

RESPONSIBILITY / TASK	Christina	Paul	Penny	Maria	Juan	H.R. Dept.	Printer
Writing			S	P	C		
Proofing	S+	S		C	P		
Editing	P	S		C			
Researching		P	S+		S		
Binding	C						P
Copying	C						P
Training	S					P	
Distribution	C					P	

Diagram # 7 - Assign strength rating

Christina directed the attention...

of the team members to the Matrix Diagram on the flip chart. She told them the next step was to assign a strength rating for each intersection of task and individual/department/supplier responsibility.

Maria was the best writer of the group, so she volunteered to take primary responsibility for the policy writing. Penny volunteered to help Maria, so she received an **S**. Juan volunteered to do the proofreading and needed to be in the *"communication loop,"* so he was given a **C** in the writing box. The rest of the group was left blank in this category. The team continued until each intersection was identified and rated with a symbol *(see Diagram # 7)....*

Decide On Next Steps

You know it's time to end the Matrix Diagram session when:

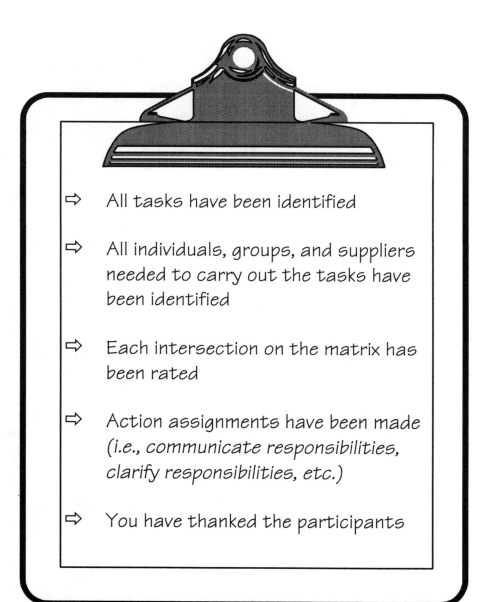

⇨ All tasks have been identified

⇨ All individuals, groups, and suppliers needed to carry out the tasks have been identified

⇨ Each intersection on the matrix has been rated

⇨ Action assignments have been made (i.e., communicate responsibilities, clarify responsibilities, etc.)

⇨ You have thanked the participants

After the team had rated all the intersections,...

they reviewed the matrix to make sure that the assignments made sense and that everyone had the time to carry out the tasks. The team then clarified exactly what each member would be doing and set the first action assignments. Christina thanked Paul, the Recorder, and called for another meeting the following Wednesday to review progress and make any necessary changes in responsibilities. She thanked the members of the team and then adjourned the meeting, confident that everything that needed to be done on the project would be taken care of and that everyone was clear on who was responsible for what.

In summary, use the Matrix Diagram when:

☑ You want to match tasks with the individuals, departments, or functions completing them. *(Often when planning we forget or omit the actual writing of the plan. The Matrix Diagram forces team members to match tasks with the individuals, departments, or functions completing them.)*

☑ You need to show a relationship between a task and the responsible person, department, or function. *(The Matrix Diagram should become a working plan that shows every implementation step and the person(s) responsible.)*

☑ You want to assign accountability and plan actions. *(Reviewing the Matrix Diagram periodically will help to hold people accountable to the plan of action.)*

CHAPTER FOUR WORKSHEET:
MATRIX DIAGRAM—IDEAS FOR USE

1. List the specific opportunities you have in your organization to use a Matrix Diagram.

_____

_____

_____

_____

_____

_____

_____

_____

2. Which of the following reasons *(or others you may think of)* for using a Matrix Diagram would apply to the situations listed above?

☐ Useful tool for communicating responsibilities

☐ Useful to ensure everything is assigned

☐ Identifies who leads and who supports

☐ Allows team members to use respective strengths and skills

☐ Improves project planning and management

FORCE FIELD DIAGRAM

The Force Field Diagram is an analysis tool your team can use when:

  ☞ **You are trying to identify obstacles to reaching a goal**

  ☞ **You are trying to identify possible causes and solutions to a problem or an important opportunity**

  ☞ **Your team is stalled in achieving its goal**

The Force Field Diagram should be used by small groups (*five to seven*) of people working toward a common goal.

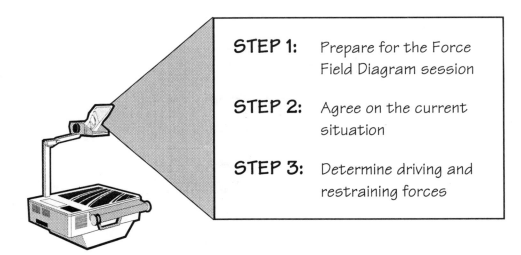

STEP 1: Prepare for the Force Field Diagram session

STEP 2: Agree on the current situation

STEP 3: Determine driving and restraining forces

The example that follows shows how using a Force Field Diagram can help during improvement activities.

> ## Sue, a Purchasing Supervisor,...
> was working with her department on reducing the amount of inventory in the warehouse. She had seen the Force Field Diagram in action and liked the way the members of a group were able to quickly determine potential obstacles as well as solutions to the issue they were tackling....

Step 1: Prepare For The Force Field Diagram Session

At the start of your Force Field session:

➠ Create a flip chart or an overhead transparency *(see Diagram # 8).*

➠ Provide a time limit to the session. Generally, setting aside 30 to 50 minutes is a good start.

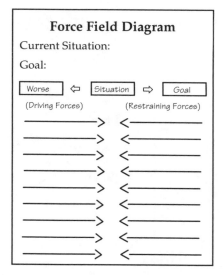

Diagram # 8 - Force Field Diagram

➠ Identify one or more Recorders. The job of the Recorder is to write down *(on a flip chart or overhead transparency)* the driving and restraining forces as they are called out.

➠ Use the ground rules of Brainstorming *(see Chapter Two).*

Sue called her department together...

for a 40-minute Force Field session covering the guidelines of how and why to use Force Field analysis. She asked Matt if he would record the group's ideas on a flip chart she had prepared for the session. Matt agreed, grabbed several markers, and the session began....

Step 2: Agree On The Current Situation

➠ The current situation simply refers to what is happening now that you want to change or improve. This is always a current issue that needs to be resolved. Write the current situation on the Force Field Diagram.

➠ If you're aware of the current situation, chances are you have an idea of your goal. Discuss with your group what the goal should be *(you may have to use Brainstorming)*. Come to agreement on the goal, and write it on the Force Field Diagram.

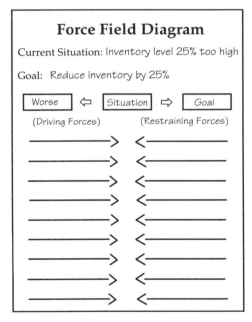

Diagram # 9 - Force Field Diagram with goal

Sue had no trouble convincing everyone...

that inventory had to be reduced; after all it was an order from the V.P. of Purchasing. After some discussion and sharing of data, they decided that the inventory level was 25 percent too high. Matt recorded this on the Force Field Diagram *(see Diagram # 9)*.

With the situation defined, the goal seemed obvious—a 25 percent reduction in the current inventory level. Sue thought, *"This is great, it only took 10 minutes to get everyone to agree. The rest should be a piece of cake."*...

Step 3: Determine Driving And Restraining Forces

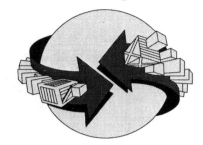

➠ **Driving forces** are things (*actions, skills, equipment, procedures, culture, people, etc.*) that help move you toward your goal. **Restraining forces** are things that can keep you from reaching your goal.

➠ As a group, ask the question, *"What things are 'driving' us toward our goal?"*

➠ The Recorder should write down the responses on the left side of the Force Field Diagram (*see Diagram # 10*). Responses are written as they are called out, with space left between each response. Continue this until all driving forces have been recorded.

➠ Then ask the question, *"What is 'restraining' us from achieving our goal?"*

➠ The Recorder then writes the responses down on the right side of the Force Field Diagram (*see Diagram # 10*). Again, responses are written as they are called out, with space left between each response. Continue this until all restraining forces have been recorded.

As the group started to call out...

the driving and restraining forces, Matt busily recorded the ideas on the flip chart. Things were starting to get a little wild, so Sue asked everyone to slow down and offer one idea at a time. The group members were excited because they were actually identifying potential obstacles or restraining forces, to reaching their goal....

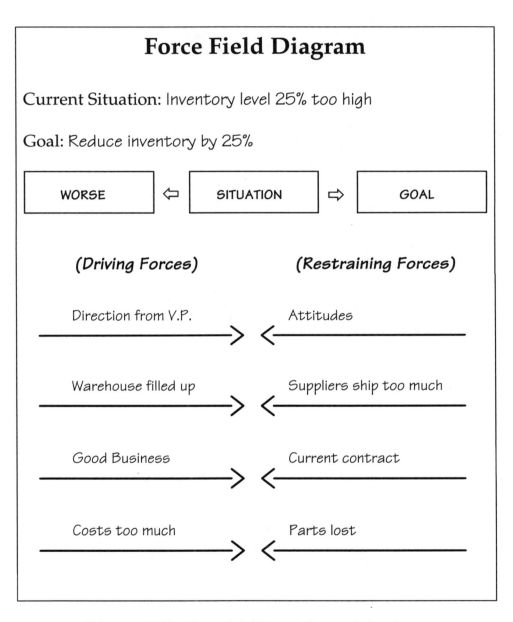

Force Field Diagram

Current Situation: Inventory level 25% too high

Goal: Reduce inventory by 25%

| WORSE | ⇦ | SITUATION | ⇨ | GOAL |

(Driving Forces) **(Restraining Forces)**

Direction from V.P.   Attitudes

Warehouse filled up   Suppliers ship too much

Good Business   Current contract

Costs too much   Parts lost

Diagram # 10 - Record driving and restraining forces

After 20 minutes,...

the group came up with 15 driving and restraining forces. Sue knew they may have missed some but felt confident that they covered the major points. After all, they were the *"experts."* They agreed the next step was to try to *"dig deeper"* for the causes of the restraining forces by asking why each one was happening *(see Diagram # 11)*. This process took 18 minutes and produced several ideas on what was causing the various restraining forces.

The team assigned an action item to several members, asking them to gather data verifying ideas on the major restraining forces. Sue thanked Matt and the team for their time. She felt confident the V.P. would respond well to their ideas about why inventory was too high.

Diagram # 11 - Ask "Why?"

Decide On Next Steps

You know it's time to end the Force Field session when:

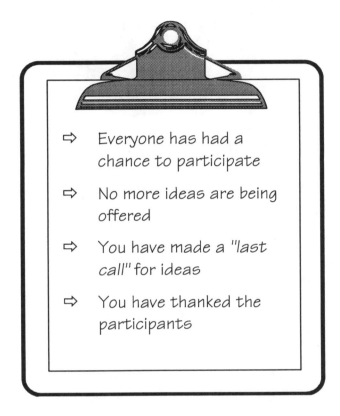

⇨ Everyone has had a chance to participate

⇨ No more ideas are being offered

⇨ You have made a "last call" for ideas

⇨ You have thanked the participants

What to do next?

➠ Your group should prioritize the driving and restraining forces. Begin to eliminate the restraining forces and capitalize on the driving forces.

➠ Your group may sort the driving and restraining forces based on common themes *(see Affinity Diagram in Chapter Three).*

➠ Your group should gather data to prove or disprove driving or restraining forces.

In summary, use the Force Field Diagram when:

☑ You are trying to identify the restraining forces in reaching a goal. *(By identifying the restraining forces, teams can determine what needs to be done to eliminate them and concentrate on the driving forces.)*

☑ You are trying to identify possible causes and solutions to a problem or an improvement opportunity. *(On the Force Field Diagram, the driving forces can act as solutions, while the restraining forces can act as causes of the problem.)*

☑ Your team is stalled in achieving its goals. *(A large portion of completing a Force Field Diagram is Brainstorming possible restraining forces. The activity of identifying them can be helpful to a team that is stalled.)*

CHAPTER FIVE WORKSHEET:
FORCE FIELD DIAGRAM—IDEAS FOR USE

1. List the specific opportunities you have in your organization to use the Force Field Diagram.

_____

_____

_____

2. What forces do you think your group will be able to identify more of, and why?

☐ Driving Forces. Why?

_____

_____

_____

_____

☐ Restraining Forces. Why?

_____

_____

_____

_____

_____

CAUSE AND EFFECT DIAGRAM

The Cause and Effect Diagram *(also known as the Fishbone Diagram)* is an analysis tool you can use to:

☞ **Categorize many potential causes of a problem or issue in an orderly way**

☞ **Analyze what is really happening in a process**

☞ **Teach teams and individuals about current or new processes and procedures**

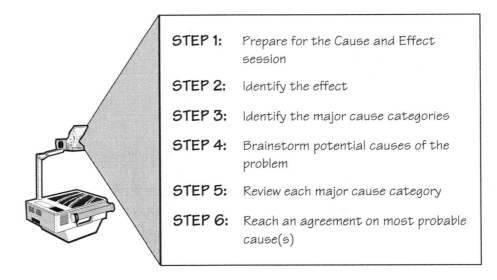

STEP 1: Prepare for the Cause and Effect session

STEP 2: Identify the effect

STEP 3: Identify the major cause categories

STEP 4: Brainstorm potential causes of the problem

STEP 5: Review each major cause category

STEP 6: Reach an agreement on most probable cause(s)

In the next example, an employee in an accounting department uses the Cause and Effect Diagram to get to the *"root cause"* of a problem.

José, an employee in the Accounting Department,...

has had enough! Once again, he turned in his budget report to his supervisor late and once again he would be criticized for his tardiness. *"What can I do?"* José asked himself. *"I don't receive my information on time, the system is always going down, and the procedure is so complex it's no wonder people are confused about what to do."* José knew his supervisor didn't want any more excuses. She wanted the problems solved and the reports on time....

Step 1: Prepare For The Cause And Effect Session

Before you begin your Cause and Effect analysis:

➠ Create a flip chart or an overhead transparency, based on the example in Diagram # 12.

➠ Provide a time limit for the session. Generally, 60 minutes is a reasonable amount of time.

➠ Identify a Recorder. The job of the Recorder is to write down *(on a flip chart or overhead transparency)* the potential causes as they are called out.

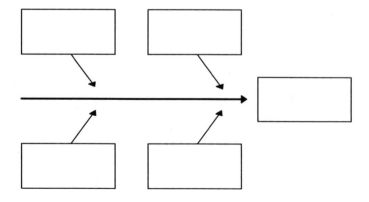

Diagram # 12 - Cause and Effect Diagram

Note: The Recorder does not necessarily decide which category the potential cause belongs in—that is a group decision.

José called his fellow employees together…

for a 60-minute meeting to get to the bottom of the problem. He decided to try the Cause and Effect Diagram, because he had heard it was a good way to get to the root cause of problems. Prior to the meeting, José made a large Cause and Effect Diagram on two pieces of flip chart paper and taped it to the wall of the conference room. He decided that for this first meeting he would be the Recorder.…

Step 2: Identify The Effect

The effect refers to the issue *(problem or process condition)* you are trying to change. Write the effect in the box on the right side of the Cause and Effect Diagram.

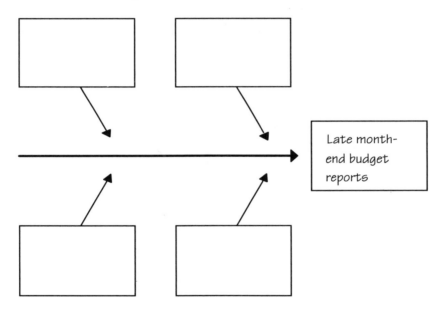

Diagram # 13 - Cause and Effect Diagram with problem identified

José began the meeting by…

reminding all those present why they were there. *"We are all having a problem getting our budget reports done on time,"* he said. *"Let's put our heads together and try to get to the bottom of this problem."* After that he wrote, *"Late month-end budget reports,"* in the box on the right side of the Cause and Effect Diagram *(see Diagram # 13).…*

Step 3: Identify The Major Cause Categories

➠ The diagonal lines that *"branch"* off the main horizontal line of the Cause and Effect Diagram are called major cause categories. You can use major cause categories to organize the causes in a way that makes the most sense for your specific situation.

You can summarize causes under categories such as:

➠ Methods, Machines, Materials, People *(the 3 M's and a P)*

➠ Places, Procedures, People, Policies *(the 4 P's)*

➠ Surroundings, Suppliers, Systems, Skills *(the 4 S's)*

Remember, these categories are only suggestions; you may use any category that helps you organize your ideas.

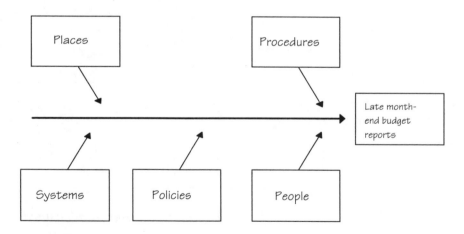

Diagram # 14 - Cause and Effect Diagram with cause categories

José wrote the 4 P's...

at the end of each of the diagonal lines. The group decided that another major cause was needed, so José added a major cause category labeled *"Systems."* *(see Diagram # 14)....*

Step 4: Brainstorm Potential Causes Of The Problem

➠ Follow the steps for Brainstorming listed in Chapter Two.

➠ As possible causes are called out, decide as a group where to place them on the Cause and Effect Diagram (*i.e., decide under which major cause category they should be placed*).

➠ It's acceptable to list a possible cause under more than one major cause category (*e.g., receiving late data could go under both People and Systems*).

➠ Try to list many possible causes on the Cause and Effect Diagram at this point.

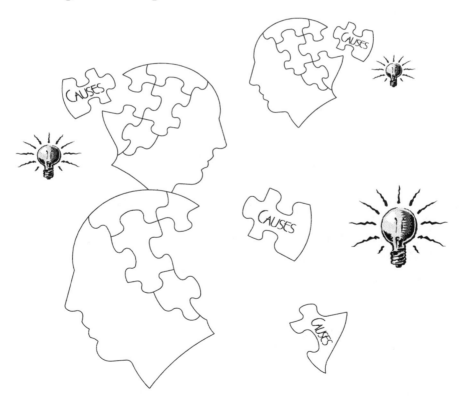

José had led Brainstorming sessions before,...

so he was familiar with the process. As the group called out each possible cause, he asked which cause category to list it under *(see Diagram #15)*. Some causes were easy, while others were more difficult to pigeonhole and ended up in two or more categories. This process continued for 25 minutes....

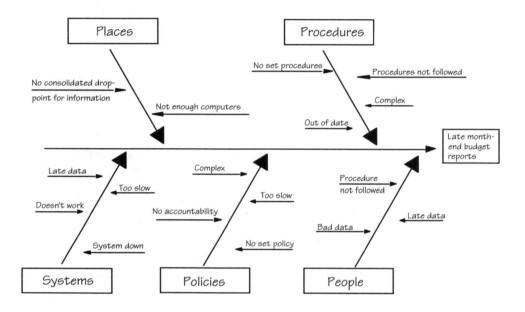

Diagram # 15 - Cause and Effect Diagram with potential causes

Step 5: Review Each Major Cause Category

➠ At this point, look for causes that appear in more than one category. This is an indication of a *"most likely cause."* Circle the most likely causes on the diagram. *(See Diagram # 16.)*

➠ Review the causes that you've circled *(the most likely causes)* and ask, *"Why is this a cause?"* Asking *"why?"* will help you get to the root cause of the problem.

➠ Record the answers to your *"why?"* questions on a separate sheet of flip chart paper.

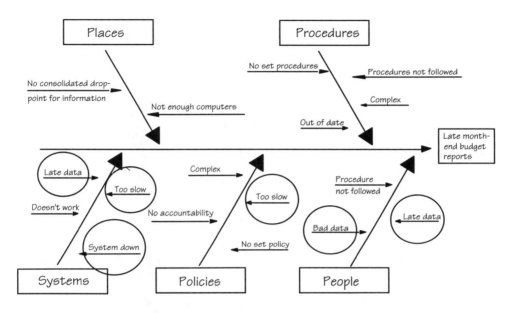

Diagram # 16 - Focus on root causes

When the group realized...

that a few of the causes appeared repeatedly (*e.g., late data, bad data, and system down*), José began asking a series of *"why"* questions (*e.g., "Why do we have late data? Why do we have bad data? Why is the system down?" etc.*). José then asked *"why?"* regarding the answers of the first questions. In doing this, the group sifted through the symptoms to get to the true root cause(s) of the problem. They felt a little uncomfortable with this process at first (*it felt a bit like an interrogation*), but soon realized they were actually getting to the root cause(s) (*see Diagram # 17*)....

Step 6: Reach An Agreement On Most Probable Cause(s)

➡ After you narrow down the most likely causes, choose from that group those you feel are the most probable causes.

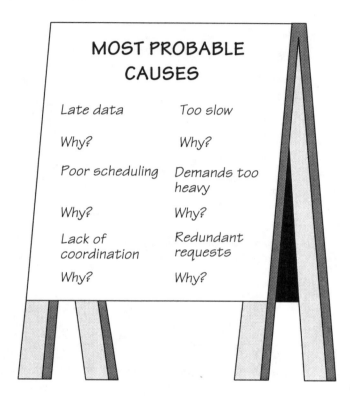

Diagram # 17 - Top two causes

After about 50 minutes,...

the group had identified what they thought were the top two most probable causes of the late report problem. The next step was to develop some type of measurement to determine whether they were right. Kim volunteered to find out how system downtime affected her ability to finish her budget report, while Marie took on the task of finding out whether procedures could be changed. José thanked all present for their time and effort and asked the team to meet at the same time the following week....

Decide On Next Steps

You know it's time to end the Cause and Effect session when:

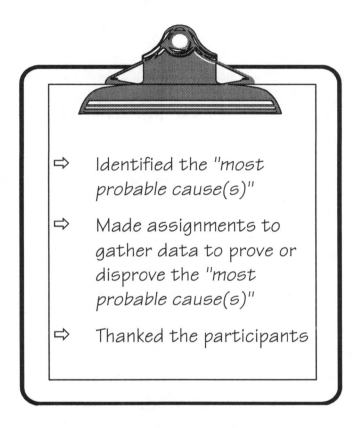

⇨ Identified the "*most probable cause(s)*"

⇨ Made assignments to gather data to prove or disprove the "*most probable cause(s)*"

⇨ Thanked the participants

SUMMARY

In summary, use the Cause and Effect Diagram when:

☑ You want to categorize many potential causes of a problem or issue in an easy-to-understand, orderly way. *(By breaking a process down into a number of process-related categories, including people, materials, machinery, procedures, policy, etc., your team is able to better identify the possible causes of a problem.)*

☑ You want to analyze what is really happening in a process *(i.e., by breaking a process down into a number of process related categories, including people, materials, machinery, procedures, policy, etc. The Cause and Effect Diagram can provide a picture of the actual process condition).*

☑ You are teaching teams and individuals about new processes and procedures *(i.e., you can use the Cause and Effect Diagram to train and/or explain how a process works).*

CHAPTER SIX WORKSHEET:
CAUSE AND EFFECT DIAGRAM—IDEAS FOR USE

1. List the specific opportunities you have in your organization to use the Cause and Effect Diagram.

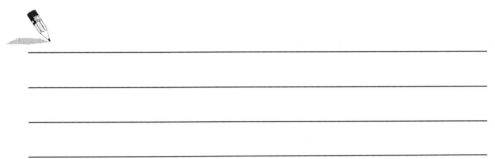

_____

_____

_____

_____

2. Identify and list which major cause categories might be appropriate for one situation you noted above.

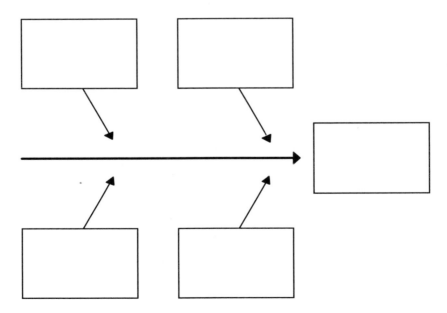

CRITERIA RATING FORM

The Criteria Rating Form is an interpretation tool you can use to select ideas and solutions from among several alternatives.

Use the Criteria Rating Form when:

☞ **You have to select among several alternatives**

☞ **You want to make a decision objectively**

☞ **You want your group to agree on a decision**

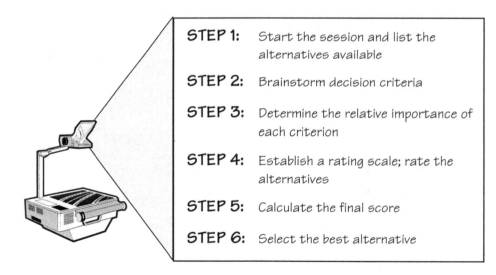

STEP 1: Start the session and list the alternatives available

STEP 2: Brainstorm decision criteria

STEP 3: Determine the relative importance of each criterion

STEP 4: Establish a rating scale; rate the alternatives

STEP 5: Calculate the final score

STEP 6: Select the best alternative

In the following example, a team is having trouble making a decision about which computer to buy.

Janet, the leader of a team...

chosen to recommend a new computer for the office, was feeling extreme pressure. Her boss was pushing the Byna 486, *Consumer Reports* recommended Quartel's 486; and to top that, most team members favored the MacGregor 4. It was already Tuesday afternoon, and Janet had to have the group's recommendations on the president's desk by Friday morning at 9:00 AM!...

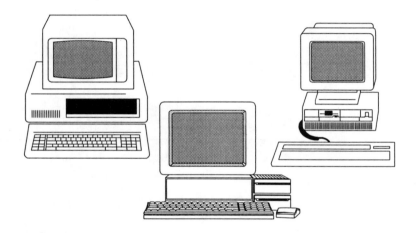

Step 1: Start The Session And List The Alternatives Available

At the start of your Criteria Rating session:

⮕ Provide a time limit for the session. Generally, 45 to 60 minutes is sufficient.

⮕ Have a Criteria Rating Form prepared on a flip chart or an overhead transparency *(see Diagram # 18)*.

⮕ List alternatives available along the top of the Criteria Rating Form.

Note: You may have to generate alternatives by Brainstorming.

First thing Wednesday morning,…

Janet called the group members into a conference room. All of them knew they had to come to an agreement on the computer choice issue. Janet suggested they use the Criteria Rating process to help them.…

CRITERIA RATING FORM

		ALTERNATIVES		
Criteria	Weight	Byna 486	Quartel 486	MacGregor 4
Total				
Summary				

Diagram # 18 - The Criteria Rating Form

Step 2: Brainstorm Decision Criteria

You will be judging your alternatives against what you feel are the most important qualities each one should have. These qualities are called decision criteria. We use decision criteria all the time. For example, when we are choosing a car to buy, we look at criteria such as cost, length of warranty, availability of service, etc. If more than one person is making the decision, it's advantageous to agree on the decision criteria. Then the decision-making process runs more smoothly.

Common criteria include:

Selection Criteria

⇨ Ease of implementation

⇨ Lowest cost

⇨ Ability to meet customer requirements

⇨ Resource availability

⇨ Lowest risk

⇨ Fastest to implement

⇨ Long-term workability

Remember, the criteria may change for each project you're working on.

➠ Your group should determine the criteria through Brainstorming. *(See Chapter Two for guidelines of Brainstorming.)*

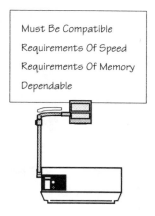

Must Be Compatible

Requirements Of Speed

Requirements Of Memory

Dependable

Janet turned on the overhead projector,...

which displayed a list she had prepared with a few of the selection criteria the group had brainstormed last week *(see Diagram # 19)*. The criteria included: new computers must be compatible with the machines the company already uses, they must be able to meet our requirements of speed and memory, and they must be dependable....

Step 3: Determine The Relative Importance Of Each Criterion

➔ Give each of the criterion a weight *(that represents its relative importance).*

➔ To determine the weight of each criterion, ask, *"How important is each of the criterion in relationship to the others?"*

➔ Remember, the total of the assigned weights for all criteria must equal 100 percent.

➔ The effectiveness of the Criteria Rating process is heavily dependent upon the weighting of the criteria. Thus, the weighting decisions must be made by a team with input from all members. For unbiased input, ask each team member to weigh the criteria individually. Determine the final weight by averaging the individual weights assigned by each team member.

		ALTERNATIVES		
Criteria	Weight	Byna 486	Quartel 486	MacGregor 4
Compatibility	40%			
Speed	20%			
Memory	20%			
Dependability	20%			
Total	100%			
Summary				

Diagram # 19 - The Criteria Rating Form with weights

Janet asked the team to review the criteria...

and decide how important each one was in relation to the others. She then asked them to assign each criterion a percentage that represented its priority, *(e.g., 10 percent would be a low priority, 70 percent would equal a high priority),* reminding everyone that the total of all the ratings must equal 100 percent. Janet gave the team five minutes to rate the list of criteria....

Step 4: Establish A Rating Scale; Rate The Alternatives

Rating Scale: **10** = high, **1** = low

Criteria	Weight	ALTERNATIVES		
		Byna 486	Quartel 486	MacGregor 4
Compatibility	40%	8	5	3
Speed	20%	4	8	6
Memory	20%	6	4	4
Dependability	20%	4	6	7
Total	100%			
Summary				

Diagram # 20 - The Criteria Rating Form with weights and ratings

➧ Your team must use consistent rating scale to compare the various alternatives against each criterion. Any scale will work as long as you use the same scale for all alternatives and criteria. An easy scale to use is 1 to 10, with 10 being high and 1 being low.

➧ Each alternative should be rated against each criterion using the established rating scale. It is possible that the rating can only be determined after an investigation (*e.g., you may have to verify which alternative has the lowest cost*).

After the team agreed...

on the weights for the criteria, they began the process of rating each of the alternatives against each criterion (*see Diagram # 20*). The Byna 486 rated highest in compatibility and memory, while the Quartel 486 and the MacGregor 4 each rated higher in speed and dependability, respectively....

Step 5: Calculate The Final Score

➠ Multiply the weight *(established in Step 3)* by the rating for each alternative *(established in Step 4)*.

➠ Write this figure in parentheses in the appropriate boxes on the Criteria Rating Form.

➠ Add the numbers in parentheses for each alternative and write the totals in the appropriate boxes.

➠ Write any summary comments in the appropriate boxes.

After a heated (but friendly) discussion,...

the group agreed on the ratings for each alternative and each criterion. Janet recorded each of the ratings directly on the Criteria Rating flip chart and asked Michael, the team math whiz *(he was the only team member with a calculator)*, to multiply each of the ratings by the weight. As Michael finished multiplying, Janet recorded the answers *(in parentheses)* on the flip chart. Michael then added each of the numbers in parentheses, and Janet wrote the final totals in the appropriate boxes on the bottom of the flip chart *(see Diagram # 21)....*

Criteria	Weight	**ALTERNATIVES**		
		Byna 486	Quartel 486	MacGregor 4
Compatibility	40%	8 x .4 (3.2)	5 x .4 (2.0)	3 x .4 (1.2)
Speed	20%	4 x .2 (.8)	8 x .2 (1.6)	6 x .2 (1.2)
Memory	20%	6 x .2 (1.2)	4 x .2 (.8)	4 x .2 (.8)
Dependability	20%	4 x .2 (.8)	6 x .2 (1.2)	7 x .2 (1.4)
Total	100%	6.0	5.6	4.6
Summary				

Diagram # 21 - The Criteria Rating Form with totals

Step 6: Select The Best Alternative

➠ Select the alternative that has the highest total score.

➠ This alternative may or may not be the one ultimately chosen. The alternative with the highest score should be the best. If the team members don't agree, they should review the weighting of the criteria and the ratings and make necessary changes.

Note: Use the summary boxes to record any notes about the alternatives.

➠ If necessary, repeat the process.

		ALTERNATIVES		
Criteria	**Weight**	Byna 486	Quartel 486	MacGregor 4
Compatibility	40%	8 x .4 (3.2)	5 x .4 (2.0)	3 x .4 (1.2)
Speed	20%	4 x .2 (.8)	8 x .2 (1.6)	6 x 2 (1.2)
Memory	20%	6 x .2 (1.2)	4 x .2 (.8)	4 x .2 (.8)
Dependability	20%	4 x .2 (.8)	6 x .2 (1.2)	7 x .2 (1.4)
Total	100%	(6.0)	5.6	4.6
Summary				

Diagram # 22 - Select the best alternative

Based on the weighting of the criteria...

and the rating of each of the alternatives, the Byna 486 had the highest total *(see Diagram # 22)*. The Quartel and the MacGregor finished second and third respectively. It was clear the Byna won because it had the highest compatibility rating, and it wasn't far behind the other models in speed, memory, and dependability. Although not everyone originally agreed on the Byna, it was hard to argue with its superiority now. After all, everyone had an equal voice in the weighting and rating process. The team had reached a true consensus....

Decide On Next Steps

You know it's time to stop the Criteria Rating session when:

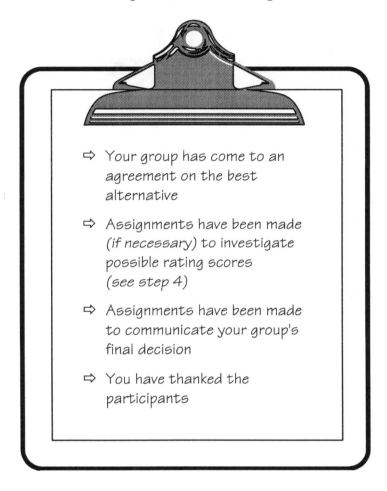

⇨ Your group has come to an agreement on the best alternative

⇨ Assignments have been made (if necessary) to investigate possible rating scores (see step 4)

⇨ Assignments have been made to communicate your group's final decision

⇨ You have thanked the participants

Since the compatibility issue was so important...

the team decided to further investigate the compatibility of the Byna 486 with the company's current machines. Denise volunteered to call Byna and verify the group's findings. She committed to having an answer by the following day. Janet and the team were happy with the results of the session. They felt confident that they could make a recommendation to the president by Friday morning.

SUMMARY

In summary, use the Criteria Rating Form when:

☑ You have to select between several alternatives. *(The Criteria Rating method will help your decision-making process by providing a step-by-step procedure.)*

☑ You want to include more objectivity into a decision-making process. *(The Criteria Rating method takes subjectivity out of the decision-making process by assigning weights and rankings to each potential solution.)*

☑ You want a consensus-building tool that will help your team reach a decision. *(The Criteria Rating method helps to build consensus by taking opinion out of the decision-making process.)*

CHAPTER SEVEN WORKSHEET:
THE CRITERIA RATING FORM—IDEAS FOR USE:

1. List the specific opportunities you have in your organization to use the Criteria Rating Form.

_____

_____

_____

2. List the criteria you might use in an upcoming situation. What weights would you assign to them?

- _____ _____ %
- _____ _____ %
- _____ _____ %
- _____ _____ %
- _____ _____ %
- _____ _____ %

100%

3. How might your choice or weighting of criteria differ if you were working on a short-term instead of a long-term issue or problem?

_____

_____

_____

_____

CHECK SHEET

Use a Check Sheet as a data-gathering and interpretation tool when you want to:

  ☞ **Distinguish between opinion and fact**

  ☞ **Gather data about how often a problem is occurring**

  ☞ **Gather data about the type of problem occurring**

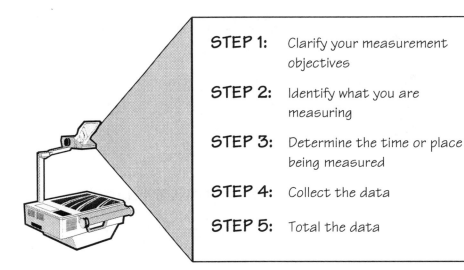

STEP 1: Clarify your measurement objectives

STEP 2: Identify what you are measuring

STEP 3: Determine the time or place being measured

STEP 4: Collect the data

STEP 5: Total the data

The following example shows how a Check Sheet can be used to distinguish between opinion and fact.

Lori had a problem....

Her department *(shipping)* was the subject of many complaints received on the company's 1-800 number. The V.P. of Operations called her into his office on Thursday and said, *"Look Lori, you have a problem with your drivers. I hear that we have been getting many complaints about late deliveries. In addition, reports show that drivers are being rude and uncooperative. What's going on here? The last thing we need is..."*

Step 1: Clarify Your Measurement Objectives

A good place to start when collecting data *(whether using a Check Sheet or not)* is to go through a process of asking some questions. Questions you should ask include:

➡ What is the problem?

➡ Why should data be collected?

➡ Who will use the information being collected and what information do they really need to see *(e.g., by department, by day, by month, by shift, by machine, etc.)*?

➡ Who will collect the data?

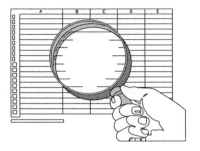

Lori agreed a problem existed...

(too many customer complaints). After all, the customers wouldn't call and make things up. And besides, the V.P. wanted some answers ASAP! Before calling the drivers in, she decided to do a little investigating. The first thing she needed to do was to collect data on the situation. Up to this point the only information she received was from the V.P. He sounded pretty sure about the drivers, but she wanted facts.

Lori was able to get a tally of complaints about shipping from the past two months. She asked the complaint monitors to keep a weekly Check Sheet of complaints for her department. Since she wanted to measure various types of complaints over a period of time and get a *"snapshot"* of the situation, she decided to make a Check Sheet of the complaint data from the previous two months....

Step 2: Identify What You Are Measuring

➠ Begin by giving your Check Sheet a title. The title should tell readers what they are looking at (*e.g., customer complaints for June, service requests for the week of..., reasons for being late to work for the month, etc.*).

➠ Next, write only the specific things you are going to measure down the left side of the Check Sheet. For example, if you are measuring customer complaints, possible categories could include late delivery, rude driver, incorrect billing, etc.

SHIPPING DEPARTMENT CUSTOMER COMPLAINTS FOR JUNE 199X

Complaint Type							
Late Delivery							
Rude Driver							
Incorrect Billing							
Wrong Delivery							
Total							

Diagram # 23 - Check Sheet with complaint types

Lori spent about an hour...

sifting through two months' worth of data. After reading through it, she decided that the complaints fell into four major categories. She named the Check Sheet *"Shipping Department Customer Complaints for June 199X"* and started filling it in *(see Diagram # 23)....*

Step 3: Determine The Time Or Place Being Measured

➤ Decide whether you want to collect information based on time *(e.g., how many things happen per hour or day)* or by place, or both *(e.g., how many things happen in department A each day, number of defects from machine B per hour, accidents by location or by month, etc.).*

Since deliveries were made Monday...

through Saturday, Lori set up her sheet with six columns *(see Diagram # 24).* She decided to tally the information by days, because she thought there might be some trends in the data *(e.g., more complaints on Monday, etc.)....*

SHIPPING DEPARTMENT CUSTOMER COMPLAINTS FOR THE FIRST WEEK OF JUNE 199X

Complaint Type	Mon 6/1/XX	Tue 6/2/XX	Wed 6/3/XX	Thur 6/4/XX	Fri 6/5/XX	Sat 6/6/XX	Total
Late Delivery							
Rude Driver							
Incorrect Billing							
Wrong Delivery							
Total							

Diagram # 24 - Blank customer complaints check sheet

Step 4: Collect The Data

➠ Begin collecting data for the items you are measuring. Record each occurrence directly on the Check Sheet as it happens. Since accuracy is essential when collecting data (*after all, you will be making decisions based on this data*), don't wait until the end of the day or when you are on a break to record information. You may forget it in the meantime.

Lori entered the information...

from the two previous months onto the Check Sheet. She was surprised by the results. It looked as if most of the complaints dealt with billing. At the end of the week, she received the current Check Sheet for her department and the results were similar (*see Diagram # 25*). She was beginning to think that maybe the V.P. had jumped to conclusions about her drivers....

SHIPPING DEPARTMENT CUSTOMER COMPLAINTS FOR THE FIRST WEEK OF JUNE 199X

Complaint Type	Mon 6/1/XX	Tue 6/2/XX	Wed 6/3/XX	Thur 6/4/XX	Fri 6/5/XX	Sat 6/6/XX	Total
Late Delivery	I	I	I I	I	I	I I	
Rude Driver	I I	I	I I I	I			
Incorrect Billing	I I I I	++++	I I I I	I I I	++++	I I I	
Wrong Delivery	I I I	I	I I	I I I	I I		
Total							

Diagram # 25 - Customer complaints for the first week of June

Step 5: Total The Data

➠ Total the number of occurrences for each category being measured *(e.g., how many times we delivered late this week, how many defects were produced by a machine today, etc.)*.

SHIPPING DEPARTMENT CUSTOMER COMPLAINTS
FOR THE FIRST WEEK OF JUNE 199X

Complaint Type	Mon 6/1/XX	Tue 6/2/XX	Wed 6/3/XX	Thur 6/4/XX	Fri 6/5/XX	Sat 6/6/XX	Total
Late Delivery	I	I	I I	I	I	I I	8
Rude Driver	I I	I	I I I	I			7
Incorrect Billing	I I I I	++++	I I I I	I I I	++++	I I I	24
Wrong Delivery	I I I	I	I I	I I I	I I I		12
Total	10	8	11	8	9	5	

Diagram # 26 - Completed customer complaints Check Sheet

After recording all the information...
on the Check Sheet, Lori added up the tally marks for each type of complaint for each day and wrote them in the appropriate boxes *(see Diagram # 26)....*

Decide On Next Steps

➠ Decide on an appropriate interpretation method.

➠ Make decisions based on fact *(not just opinion)* about what you are measuring. Since you have data, you can decide how to begin making needed improvements.

➠ Continue to collect data to verify your original findings and to evaluate any changes *(improvements)* you make.

After reviewing the weekly data...

on complaints for a month, Lori felt confident that billing errors accounted for the majority of customer complaints. Her meeting with the V.P. of Operations was scheduled for the next day, and she was going to be armed with the Check Sheets from the past four weeks. *"Even he,"* she thought, *"couldn't argue with this data."* She also knew that if changes were going to be made in billing, more information would be needed, so she continued to collect the weekly data on customer complaints.

SUMMARY

In summary, use the Check Sheet when you want to ...

☑ Distinguish between opinion and fact. *(We often think we know which problem, or underlying cause is most important. The Check Sheet helps to prove or disprove those opinions.)*

☑ Gather data about how often a problem is occurring. *(The main purpose of the Check Sheet is to help tabulate the number of occurrences of a given problem or cause.)*

☑ Gather data about the type of problem that is occurring. *(Check Sheets help you break down data into different categories such as causes, problems, etc.)*

CHAPTER EIGHT WORKSHEET:
CHECK SHEETS—IDEAS FOR USE

1. List the specific opportunities you have in your organization to use Check Sheets.

_____

_____

_____

_____

2. Out of the situations you listed above, which one represents a pressing issue that needs to be taken care of soon? Why?

_____

_____

_____

3. What type of data might you collect with the Check Sheet in this situation?

_____

_____

_____

_____

SUMMARY

Consider your quality-improvement effort as you would a construction job, such as building a house. You can assemble enthusiastic and able professionals, purchase the best building supplies available, even contract a renowned architect to design your house; but, if you don't have the right tools for the job, all your effort is wasted.

This analogy is appropriate for your own construction job—improving quality on or off the job. You need the right tools—Brainstorming, the Affinity Diagram, the Force Field Diagram, the Matrix Diagram, the Cause and Effect Diagram, the Criteria Rating Form, and the Check Sheet—and you need to know how to use them correctly. This knowledge is essential to *"building"* your quality-improvement effort.

For any tool to be effective, you need to know how and when to apply it. Each tool presented in this guidebook is used in a different situation. For example, Brainstorming, the Affinity Diagram, and the Matrix Diagram are planning tools. The Force Field Diagram and the Cause and Effect Diagram are both analysis tools. The Criteria Rating Form is a planning tool, and the Check Sheet is an analysis tool. Both are also interpretation tools. See the Selection Matrix in Chapter One for a quick reference of the uses of all the tools in this guidebook and *Continuous Improvement Tools Volume 2*. Just as a hammer, a screw driver, and a saw are used for different jobs, quality tools all have different primary functions as well.

We are all in the position to improve our jobs. The smallest of individual efforts can *(and often does)* add up to large organizational improvements. The examples used in this guidebook show how teams and individuals can use the tools *(as carpenters or cabinetmakers use the tools of their trade)* to "build" real improvements into their immediate jobs. By using these tools, you too can make a difference by building quality into your organization.

REPRODUCIBLE FORMS
AND WORKSHEETS

The pages in the Appendix are provided for you to photocopy and use appropriately.

MATRIX DIAGRAM WORKSHEET

Address the following questions when preparing to use a Matrix Diagram.

1. Determine the level at which you are defining the tasks. *(For each task, there may be subtasks, which may in turn have additional subtasks.)*

_____

_____

_____

2. Define the specific outcome(s) of your project *(e.g., the specific, tangible, and intangible outcomes such as a report, a presentation, equipment installation, etc.).*

_____

_____

_____

3. List all the tasks that you need to complete to achieve your desired outcome(s).

_____

_____

_____

4. Do all the group members agree on the criteria for matching the tasks with the appropriate people *(e.g., time, expertise, learning opportunities, etc.)*? List any disagreements.

_____

_____

_____

_____

_____

_____

_____

5. Do all group members understand the connection between their tasks and the tasks of others they have to pass along their part of the project to?

_____

_____

_____

_____

_____

_____

MATRIX DIAGRAM

RESPONSIBILITY / TASK									

FORCE FIELD DIAGRAM WORKSHEET

Address the following questions when preparing to use a Force
Field Diagram.

1. Describe the current situation. Is this definition agreed to by all
involved?

_____

_____

_____

_____

2. List the data supporting this definition of the current situation.

_____

_____

_____

_____

3. Describe the goal. Is there agreement on it?

_____

_____

_____

_____

FORCE FIELD DIAGRAM

Current Situation:

Goal:

| Worse | ⇐ | Situation | ⇨ | Goal |

(Driving Forces)   (Restraining Forces)

———————>   <———————
———————>   <———————
———————>   <———————
———————>   <———————
———————>   <———————
———————>   <———————
———————>   <———————
———————>   <———————
———————>   <———————

CAUSE AND EFFECT
DIAGRAM WORKSHEET

Address the following questions when preparing to use the Cause and Effect Diagram:

1. Describe the issue or effect of the problem. Has it been clearly defined and agreed to?

_____

_____

_____

_____

2. List the major cause categories you will use.

_____

_____

_____

_____

3. Describe the process you will use to narrow down the list of possible causes your group comes up with.

_____

_____

_____

4. How will you get to the true root cause of the shorter list of probable causes your group will develop?

5. Is your group going to be prepared to take on assignments to gather data or handle follow-up tasks? How will this be done?

CAUSE AND EFFECT DIAGRAM

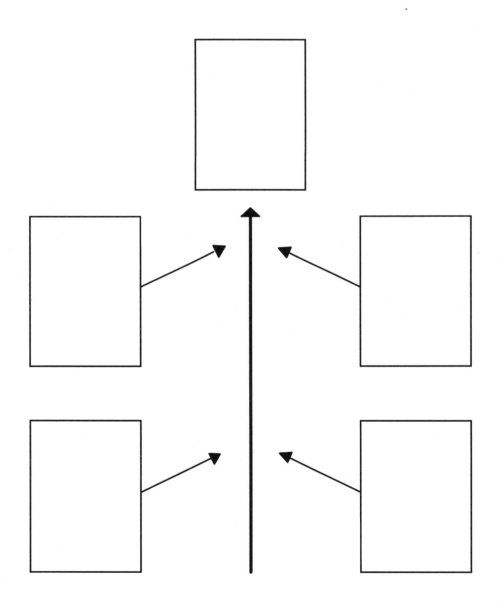

CRITERIA RATING FORM WORKSHEET

Address the following questions when preparing to use the Criteria Rating Form:

1. Have you narrowed down your list of alternatives to a manageable number—approximately six or less? Or, if necessary, have you agreed on a process to help you arrive at a relatively short list? Write down your short list.

_____

_____

_____

_____

_____

2. Do you have the right criteria to fit the specific situation you are working with? List your criteria.

_____

_____

_____

_____

_____

_____

_____

3. Has everyone involved come to a consensus on the weighting of the criteria? If not, why?

_____

_____

_____

_____

4. Does the alternative with the highest score seem to be the best choice? Why or why not?

_____

_____

_____

_____

5. What do you need to address in a follow-up plan?

_____

_____

_____

_____

_____

_____

CRITERIA RATING FORM

Criteria	Weight	ALTERNATIVES		
Total				
Summary				

CHECK SHEET WORKSHEET

Address the following questions when preparing to use the Check Sheet:

1. Are others who may be affected aware of why you are gathering information and how it will be used?

_____

_____

_____

2. Identify what information you will gather.

_____

_____

_____

3. How will you compare this information to information from other time periods?

_____

_____

_____

_____

4. How will you interpret the data on the Check Sheet *(e.g., by using a Pareto Chart)*?

_____

_____

_____

_____

_____

_____

5. How will you communicate the data and the conclusions drawn from it?

_____

_____

_____

_____

_____

_____

_____

CHECK SHEET

							Total
Total							

PROFESSIONAL AND PERSONAL DEVELOPMENT PUBLICATIONS FROM RICHARD CHANG ASSOCIATES, INC.

Designed to support continuous learning, these highly targeted, integrated collections from Richard Chang Associates, Inc. (RCA) help individuals and organizations acquire the knowledge and skills needed to succeed in today's ever-changing workplace. Titles are available through RCA, Jossey-Bass, Inc., fine bookstores, and distributors internationally.

PRACTICAL GUIDEBOOK COLLECTION

QUALITY IMPROVEMENT SERIES
Continuous Process Improvement
Continuous Improvement Tools, Volume 1
Continuous Improvement Tools, Volume 2
Step-By-Step Problem Solving
Meetings That Work!
Improving Through Benchmarking
Succeeding As A Self-Managed Team
Measuring Organizational Improvement Impact
Process Reengineering In Action
Satisfying Internal Customers First!

MANAGEMENT SKILLS SERIES
Interviewing And Selecting High Performers
On-The-Job Orientation And Training
Coaching Through Effective Feedback
Expanding Leadership Impact
Mastering Change Management
Re-Creating Teams During Transitions
Planning Successful Employee Performance
Coaching For Peak Employee Performance
Evaluating Employee Performance

HIGH PERFORMANCE TEAM SERIES
Success Through Teamwork
Building A Dynamic Team
Measuring Team Performance
Team Decision-Making Techniques

HIGH-IMPACT TRAINING SERIES
Creating High-Impact Training
Identifying Targeted Training Needs
Mapping A Winning Training Approach
Producing High-Impact Learning Tools
Applying Successful Training Techniques
Measuring The Impact Of Training
Make Your Training Results Last

WORKPLACE DIVERSITY SERIES
Capitalizing On Workplace Diversity
Successful Staffing In A Diverse Workplace
Team Building For Diverse Work Groups
Communicating In A Diverse Workplace
Tools For Valuing Diversity

PERSONAL GROWTH AND DEVELOPMENT COLLECTION

Managing Your Career in a Changing Workplace
Unlocking Your Career Potential
Marketing Yourself and Your Career
Making Career Transitions
Memory Tips For The Forgetful

101 STUPID THINGS COLLECTION

101 Stupid Things Trainers Do To Sabotage Success
101 Stupid Things Supervisors Do To Sabotage Success
101 Stupid Things Employees Do To Sabotage Success
101 Stupid Things Salespeople Do To Sabotage Success
101 Stupid Things Business Travelers Do To Sabotage Success

About Richard Chang Associates, Inc.

Richard Chang Associates, Inc. (RCA) is a multi-disciplinary organizational performance improvement firm. Since 1987, RCA has provided private and public sector clients around the world with the experience, expertise, and resources needed to build capability in such critical areas as process improvement, management development, project management, team performance, performance measurement, and facilitator training. RCA's comprehensive package of services, products, and publications reflect the firm's commitment to practical, innovative approaches and to the achievement of significant, measurable results.

RCA Resources Optimize Organizational Performance

Consulting — Using a broad range of skills, knowledge, and tools, RCA consultants assist clients in developing and implementing a wide range of performance improvement initiatives.

Training — Practical, "real world" training programs are designed with a "take initiative" emphasis. Options include off-the-shelf programs, customized programs, and public and on-site seminars.

Curriculum And Materials Development — A cost-effective and flexible alternative to internal staffing, RCA can custom-develop and/or customize content to meet both organizational objectives and specific program needs.

Video Production — RCA's award-winning, custom video productions provide employees with information in a consistent manner that achieves lasting impact.

Publications — The comprehensive and practical collection of publications from RCA supports organizational training initiatives and self-directed learning.

Packaged Programs — Designed for first-time and experienced trainers alike, these programs offer comprehensive, integrated materials (including selected Practical Guidebooks) that provide a wide range of flexible training options. Choose from:

- Meetings That Work! ToolPAK™
- Step-By-Step Problem Solving ToolKIT™
- Continuous Process Improvement Packaged Training Program
- Continuous Improvement Tools, Volume 1 ToolPAK™
- Continuous Improvement Tools, Volume 2 ToolPAK™
- High Involvement Teamwork™ Packaged Training Program

RICHARD
CHANG
ASSOCIATES

World Class Resources. World Class Results.^{SM}

Richard Chang Associates, Inc.
Corporate Headquarters
15265 Alton Parkway, Suite 300, Irvine, California 92618 USA
(800) 756-8096 • (949) 727-7477 • Fax: (949) 727-7007
E-Mail: info@rca4results.com • www.richardchangassociates.com

U.S. Offices in Irvine and Atlanta • Licensees and Distributors Worldwide